W9-BEJ-826

Bannockburn School Dist. 106
2165 Telegraph Road
Bannockburn, Illinois 60015

DATE DUE

DEC 03 2009			
JAN 26 2010			

HIGHSMITH 45231

HOW DOES IT GROW?

DUCK

by Jinny Johnson
Illustrations by Michael Woods

A+
Smart Apple Media

Bannockburn School Dist. 106
2165 Telegraph Road
Bannockburn, Illinois 60015

Smart Apple Media
P.O. Box 3263, Mankato, MN 56002

U.S. publication copyright © 2010 Smart Apple Media. International copyright reserved in all countries. No part of this book may be reproduced in any form without written permission from the publisher.

Printed in the United States of America

Library of Congress Cataloging-in-Publication Data

Johnson, Jinny.
  Duck / Jinny Johnson ; illustrations by Michael Woods.
     p. cm. -- (How does it grow?)
  Includes index.
  ISBN 978-1-59920-353-9 (hardcover)
  1. Ducks--Life cycles--Juvenile literature. I. Woods, Michael, 1943- ill. II. Title.
  QL696.A52J64 2010
  598.4'1156--dc22
                                                2008053338

All words in **bold** can be found in the glossary on page 30.

Designed by Helen James
Edited by Mary-Jane Wilkins
Picture research by Su Alexander

Photograph acknowledgements
page 7 E R Degginger/Photolibrary Group; 17 Peter Bisset/Photolibrary Group;
23 Elliott Neep/Photolibrary Group; 29 Ronald Wittek/Photolibrary Group
Front cover Ronald Wittek/Photolibrary Group

9 8 7 6 5 4 3 2 1

Contents

What's Inside?

These cream-colored eggs
have been laid by a **mallard** duck.
Inside each egg a tiny baby duckling
is beginning to grow.

There are 10 eggs in this **nest**.
The nest is made of twigs.
The mother duck has lined the
inside with leaves, grass, and soft
feathers from her body.

The eggs need to be kept warm
and safe until they **hatch**.

Mallard ducks lay
between 8 and 13 eggs
each spring.

4

Who looks after the eggs?

Keeping Warm

The mother duck looks after
the eggs. She sits on the nest
and keeps the eggs warm
with her body.

The mother turns the eggs
regularly, using her **beak** and her
feet. She makes sure that every
part of the egg stays warm.

She leaves the nest only twice a
day. Once in the morning and once
in the afternoon, she goes to find
food. Before she leaves, she covers
the eggs so they don't get cold.

THE MOTHER DUCK'S
FEATHERS HELP HER
BLEND INTO THE
SURROUNDINGS.

How long before the eggs hatch?

Ready to Hatch

About four weeks after
the eggs have been laid,
they are ready to hatch.

A day or two before the eggs
hatch, the ducklings start to chirp
and squeak inside the eggs. The
mother calls quietly back. She
stays close and doesn't leave her
eggs at any moment.

Soon a little crack appears
in an egg. The first duckling
is about to hatch.

THE MOTHER DUCK
WATCHES OVER THE
EGGS AS THE FIRST
ONE BEGINS TO HATCH.

How does a duckling get out of the egg?

Breaking Out

The duckling has to break free
of its shell on its own. It's not easy.
The duckling has a hard tip on its
beak, called an **egg tooth**, that
it uses to peck its way out.

Once one egg starts to hatch,
the others soon follow. As each
duckling struggles out, it snuggles
under its mom's warm body.

Hatching is hard work and
the ducklings need to rest.

ALL THE EGGS
USUALLY HATCH
ON THE SAME DAY.

What does the baby duckling look like?

First Day

The newly hatched duckling is covered with soft yellow and brown fluffy **down**. It's damp and sticky at first and takes about half a day to dry.

The duckling soon starts to move around the nest. He's steadier on his legs now, but still stays close to mom.

Some of the special oil on the mother duck's feathers rubs off on her ducklings. This oil makes their downy coats waterproof.

THE DUCKLINGS ARE FLUFFY
AND STAY CLOSE TOGETHER.

When will the ducklings go for their first walk?

Leaving the Nest

The day after they hatch,
the ducklings leave the nest
for the first time.

The mom leads her line of
fluffy ducklings to the water.
She calls to them all the time
and makes sure they stay in line.

When they reach the water,
it's time for their first swim.

THE DUCKLINGS
MUST BE CAREFUL
NOT TO GET LEFT
BEHIND.

Can the ducklings swim right away?

Learning to Swim

The ducklings take a little while to get used to swimming, but soon they are bobbing about on the water. They paddle with their **webbed feet**.

The ducklings can find their own food on their first swim. They snap up tiny insects and water plants with their broad, flat beaks.

For the first week or so, the mother snuggles up with her ducklings at night. She keeps them warm with her body.

THE DUCKLINGS SWIM IN A GROUP, WITH THE MOTHER DUCK AS THEIR LEADER.

Do the ducklings still need their mom?

Staying Safe

The ducklings need their mom to keep them safe. She makes sure they all stay close together. If any wander too far away, she **quacks** loudly to call them back.

The ducklings can't fly yet, so it is hard for them to escape from danger, especially when they feed on land. They scuttle around, eating seeds, worms, and snails. They may leap up to grab insects from the air or from plants.

When they are a few weeks old, the ducklings start to lose their fluffy down and grow adult feathers.

THE DUCKLINGS STAY CLOSE TOGETHER AS THEY HUNT FOR SMALL THINGS TO EAT.

When will the ducklings be able to fly?

Learning to Fly

By the time they are eight or nine weeks old, the ducklings start to look more and more like their parents. Their wings have grown bigger and they are ready to fly.

A duckling flaps its wings, copying how it has seen its mother flap hers. It takes a few tries to fly, but soon the duckling is in the air.

Now they can fly and look after themselves. Ducklings usually leave their mother once they can fly.

THE DUCK FLAPS ITS WINGS AND PADDLES ITS FEET TO FLY OUT OF THE WATER.

What do the ducks do all day?

A Duck's Day

The ducks spend their days
feeding, bathing, sleeping,
and cleaning their feathers.

They are strong fliers and can
fly up from the water as well
as from land. They are good
swimmers and can tip upside
down when they look for food.

The male ducks look very different
from females when they are full
grown. They have shiny green
feathers on their heads
and reddish-brown chests.

A MALE DUCK IS
CALLED A **DRAKE**.

When do ducks start their own family?

Finding a Mate

When ducks are about nine months old, it is time for them to start their own family.

Male ducks must show off to females and attract a mate. Females like males that have bright yellow beaks and glossy feathers.

Once a male duck has found a female, they swim and feed together. A mallard duck feeds by dipping its head down, sticking its bottom up, and fishing for food in the water. In spring, the pair will **mate**.

THE MALE AND FEMALE
DUCK BOND TOGETHER
BY SEARCHING FOR FOOD
UNDER THE WATER.

Who makes the nest?

A New Family

The female mallard duck prepares her nest. She lays her first egg and covers it up with grass and feathers. Every day she lays another egg until she has a **clutch**.

Laying eggs is tiring. Her mate stays close by to help protect her while she lays eggs, but then he leaves.

The soon-to-be mom settles down to look after her eggs until her new duckling family is ready to hatch.

THE FEMALE LAYS THE WHOLE CLUTCH BEFORE SHE STARTS TO SIT ON HER EGGS.

More About Ducks

What is the mallard duck related to?

A mallard spends some of its time on land and some in water. It is related to other water-living birds, such as geese, swans, and other ducks. There are lots of other kinds of ducks, but the mallard is the most common. There are more mallards in the world than any other kind of duck.

Where do mallards live?

Mallards originally lived in North America, Europe, and Asia, but now they have spread to many other parts of the world. They are very adaptable and are happy to live in parks, in the middle of busy cities, and in the country.

How big is a mallard?

A full-grown mallard duck is 20 to 26 inches (50 to 65 cm) long and weighs up to 3 pounds (1.4 kg). When its wings are fully spread, they measure up to 3 feet (95 cm) from tip to tip.

Female and male mallards look quite different.

The brown coloring of the female helps her hide when she's sitting on the nest.

Words to Remember

beak
the hard outer part of a bird's mouth

clutch
a group of eggs laid by a bird

down
a bird's first soft feathers

drake
a male mallard

egg tooth
a little spike on a baby bird's beak that is used to break out of the egg; it falls off a few days after hatching.

hatch
to break out of an egg

mallard
a common wild duck that lives in North America, Europe, and Northern Asia

mate
Male and female animals pair up, or mate, to produce young. An animal's partner is called its mate.

nest

a place where a bird lays its eggs

quack

the sound made by a female mallard duck

webbed feet

feet with flaps of skin between the toes that help the duck move in water

Web Sites

For Students
National Geographic Mallard Duck Profile
http://animals.nationalgeographic.com/animals/birds/
mallard-duck.html

Texas Parks and Wildlife Information on Mallard Ducks
http://www.tpwd.state.tx.us/kids/wild_things/birds/mallard.phtml

For Teachers
Earth Care Lesson Plan on Mallard Ducks
http://www.earthcarecanada.com/EarthCARE_Resources/
Ducklings.asp

The Junior Duck Stamp Program (Teaching Conservation)
http://www.calwaterfowl.org/duck_stamp/resources.htm

Index